THE GRECO-PERSIAN WARS

by The Nueva School 4th Grade Class 2018

The Greco-Persian Wars by The Nueva School Fourth Grade Class of 2017-2018
Published by The Nueva School, 6565 Skyline Blvd., Hillsborough, California 94010
www.nuevaschool.org
© 2018 The Nueva School

Front cover by Caleb, Emi
Back cover by Eliza, Madison

Contents

Introduction

Our first theme in this book is the story of David vs. Goliath, which is a story about a victory of small over big. There was a shepherd named David and a mighty warrior named Goliath. They were each in a different army. Goliath's army was heading to attack the town that David lived in. The two sides agreed to choose one champion for their army to fight the champion from the other army. Goliath's army easily chose him, but everyone in the other army was afraid to fight him. Finally, David volunteered to face Goliath. Since he was so small, he didn't want to fight in close combat with a sword, so he picked up a sling to use for his weapon. He went down into the valley with his sling and a stone, swung it around his head, and let the stone go with all his might. The stone hit Goliath right on his head and killed him. The David vs. Goliath story is significant to the Greco-Persian Wars because Greece was a bunch of small city-states that squabbled with each other, but Persia was a giant empire.

The second theme is Freedom vs. Totalitarianism. Totalitarianism means ruled by one person. It can sometimes be sufficient, depending on how good the ruler is. Freedom offers more choice, but there are still rules, and the citizens can say no to their rulers. Freedom vs. Totalitarianism is significant to the Greco-Persian Wars because Persia was an empire ruled by one man, but Greece was a bunch of separate city-states, each of which had their own rules, and some of them had Democracy.

The third theme is the beginning of Western history. It was the start of many of the things we have today, such as philosophy, art, music, drama, Democracy, and lots more. If the war had gone differently, our world today would be very different too.

Herodotus was the first historian and was the father of history. He wrote about the Greco-Persian Wars. Most of the knowledge we have now about the Greco-Persian Wars is from Herodotus.

1

Greeks and Persians

Persia's first major king was named Cyrus. Cyrus was a glorious Persian conqueror who expanded Persia to a third of the known world. Before Cyrus the Great, Persia was just a teeny little place in the middle of nowhere that was conquered by the Medes, which is where Iran is now. Cyrus raised an army and conquered the Medes, all his neighbors, conquered his neighbor's neighbors, and so on. In doing so he made Persia a world power. Cyrus reigned from 559-530 BCE. First, he conquered the Lydian Empire because his camels smelled weird to the Lydian king's horses, which scared them, and he went on to expand into the Neo-Babylonian Empire. He died fighting the Massagetae tribe.

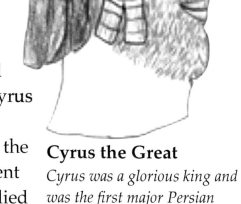

Cyrus the Great
Cyrus was a glorious king and was the first major Persian emperor.

His son, Cambyses II conquered Egypt, Nubia, and Cyrenaica, before he failed to take over Ethiopia. While he was marching back to Persia, his army withered away in a sand storm in Lydia. He died in 530 BCE while going to crush a rebellion.

Cambyses II's successor, Darius, started the Greco-Persian war by taking over the Greek colonies of Ionia. Darius, being Cambyses' closest relative, his cousin, got the throne after Cambyses died. As soon as he took over, a rebel group attacked, thinking he could be weak. Unfortunately for them, he sent the army in and coldly and calmly killed them all.

Cyrus's Palace
This is a picture of Cyrus the Great's palace.

It is hard to find the first Greek king, although they probably started off in Crete, but some major Greek leaders are the following: Minos, Themistocles, Lycaus, Leonidas, Alexander the Great, and Pericles.

Hippias

Hippias was a Greek king before the Greco-Persian Wars.

Empire Word Study

Em + pire → Empire

Definition: A group of countries ruled by a single authority.

Part of speech: Noun

Root: Latin: *Parare*

Denotation: "To order, prepare"

Related words: disparate, imperative, prepare

Persian Weapons

Spear: The Persian spear was six feet long with a broad leaf-shaped head. When used overhand it could stab down and hit the heart when the soldiers were the same height, but if one was significantly taller it could hit his head. If one soldier was shorter than his opponent he could use the spear underhand so that he could stab up.

Bow and Arrow: The bow was long range and considered cowardly by the Spartans and other Greeks because they thought you were a coward if you fought at long range. The Persian archers were partly Ethiopian. At the Battle of Thermopylae the Persian archers killed all the Greeks who were alive after the Immortals' charge.

Sword: A Shamshir was a sword used by the Persians with a giant curve. Unlike the Khopesh, whose blade went in and then out, a Shamshir blade just went out.

Map of Greece Before the Persian Wars

Cyrus the Great

Cyrus was the founder of the Achaemenid empire, the first Persian empire. He created the largest empire the world had ever seen. He had seven titles, including The Great King and King of the Four Corners of the World. He conquered the Median Empire first, the Lydian Empire second, and finally the Neo-Babylonian empire.

He died in battle fighting the Massagetae along the Syr Darya in December 530 BCE. His reign was around 30 years long. Cyrus's grandfather was Cyrus I, his father was Cambyses I, he was Cyrus II, and his son was Cambyses II.

More Greeks and Persians

Persian Immortal

These are the special soldiers that the Persians had.

The Greco-Persian Wars were a big deal. Seriously. We think the Greeks were so great, but really the Persians had a bigger navy and a bigger army. So, in other words, the Persians were pretty much superior to the Greeks.

Greeks only had heavy infantry, whereas the Persians had light infantry, cavalry (it was a big advantage at the time), and archers. The Greeks had a three-foot decorative shield called a *hoplon* for scaring the other side, a helmet, a strong chest plate, and a pair of calf guards. They used an eight-foot spear and a shorter stabbing sword. These soldiers were called *hoplites* after their shields.

The Persians had special soldiers called Immortals, so called because every time the Greeks killed one of them, there would always be another one to take his place. The Immortals wore long cloaks and their weapons were a short stabbing sword and a spear. Persian soldiers wore sandals, a light cloak, and at their sides were a couple of daggers. Cavalry had pretty much the same thing as Greek hoplites. Archers wore leather pants, leather shirts, a quiver of arrows, and they held deadly bows.

The Greeks also had a formation called the *phalanx,* where each soldier put his shield on his left side and the soldier on his left's right. This left the right side of a phalanx weak, so the Greek commanders took special care to protect it. This strategy was very effective, and the hoplites got extremely good at this. They could turn, run, back up, or do pretty much anything else in phalanx formation. This was quite impressive because the Greek armor weighed seventy pounds, and they had to do it all together in perfect formation, because otherwise they would fall apart and their long spears would impale their comrades.

Greeks and Persians thought of each other as barbarians. The Greeks wore tunics and the Persians wore shirts and pants. They each thought the others' clothing and way of living and battle strategies were barbaric, because they were different from their own culture.

Squabbling Greeks

Greek city-states were always squabbling with each other. Athens and Sparta were the most common city-states to squabble. This led to three things: the Peloponnesian War, which is also called the Suicide of Greece, the end of the world-changing Golden Age, and the second downfall of Athens.

Greek Armor

This is the standard Greek armor that warriors fought in. It was very heavy and hot, and it was the same for every soldier. Imagine walking and running miles carrying 70 lbs., and that's not even the fighting part. The helmets sometimes had feathers or horsehair to look fashionable.

Breast Plate

Greek Shield

This type of Greek shield was called a hoplon.

Leg guard

Helmet

Immortal Word Study

Im + mort + al → Immortal
Definition: Living forever, never dying
Part of speech: Noun or adjective
Root: Latin: *Mortus*
Denotation: "To die"
  Related words: mortify, mortgage, Voldemort

The Phalanx

Imagine a wall of spears coming at you. There are ten columns and ten rows of warriors. The back five rows have their spears pointed up in the air. The front five have their spears pointed right at you. The one-meter wide shields cover half of the body of the warrior holding them and half of the person on their left, but the warriors that are on the farthest right are vulnerable because they can get stabbed on their sides. That's what a phalanx is.

Persian Empire Map

This is what the Persian Empire looked like after Cyrus's death.

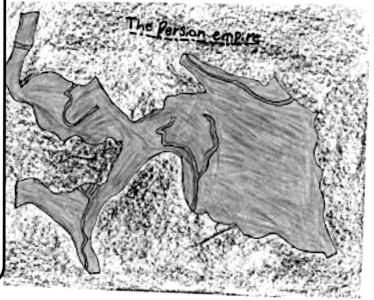

The Persian empire

The Ionian Revolt

The Ionian Revolt started when Darius I (the Persian king) took control of some Greek colonies, and it ended up lasting for six years. The Ionians weren't happy, so they revolted against the great Persian Empire. The first thing they did was send Aristagoras to ask Sparta to help them with their revolt, because Sparta was the most powerful city state in Greece. It was hard for Aristagoras because he had to convince two kings (Sparta had two kings, Cleomenes I and Leonidas, who made all the decisions). The kings asked him how long the journey would take.

Aristagoras said, "Four months."

"No way. Get out of Sparta by dusk or we'll kill you!" the kings exclaimed.

Then Aristagoras went to Athens. Since Athens was a democracy, he had to convince a crowd, and it was easier to convince a crowd because he could use speeches and get them all excited. He went to Athens and the archon (the leader of Athens) agreed to let him make a speech in public. Athens agreed because a lot of people wanted to get the loot that they would get if they won.

Athens sent twenty triremes to Ionia, defeated and sacked one town, got lots of loot, and left. Afterwards, Ionia was overpowered and defeated by the Persian Empire.

Every night at a dinner, a servant told Darius, "Remember the Athenians, sire." This inspired Persia to attack Greece a few years later, and to target Athens first.

Samos

While Persia was defeating Ionia it had a problem. There was an Ionian fortress called Samos that they wanted to conquer. The problem was that Samos was half a mile out to sea so they couldn't use their army. Also, they couldn't use their navy because Samos had a bigger navy than Persia had in that area. Darius decided to invite the leader of the fortress, Polycrates, out to talk about peace. They crucified him, which means nailing him to a cross with iron spikes and waiting for him to die from hypoxia (running out of oxygen), and the people in Samos surrendered.

Revolt Word Study

Re + volt → Revolt
Definition: "Rebel(lion) against"
Part of speech: Verb or noun
Root: Latin: *Volvere*
Denotation: "To roll"
Related words: revolve, revolution, devolve

Sacking a Town

Sacking was a way to completely demolish a city or town. Usually it involved burning and taking everything in the intended target. The people sacking the city were usually looking for gold, fame, and slaves. A lot of citizens were killed and people had to flee. Homes and temples were burned and destroyed. Football adopted this term because sacking the quarterback means you tackle him behind the line of scrimmage.

Trireme

Triremes (called this because of the three rows of oars) were the Greek ultimate battle ships. They were 120 feet long and it took 170 men to operate the oars. They had a 440 pound bronze ram in the front of the boat and supports to hold the ram in place, just below water level. They had two sails, which enabled them to go as fast as 7.5 knots (8.6 mph). The sails could be stripped down for battle and the rowers would take control. By oar power it could go ten knots (11.5 mph) in short bursts. Triremes were usually used in battle for ramming other ships in their sides, and sending their soldiers onto the other ship.

Croesus of Lydia

In 595 BCE, a little boy was born, named Croesus. He had one sibling named Aryenis, born in 598 BCE. Their father was Alyattes of Lydia. Croesus grew up to be king of Lydia. According to Herodotus, his reign lasted for fourteen years, starting in 560 BCE until he was defeated by Cyrus the Great, King of Persia, in 546 BCE. He died the next year, which was 545 BCE. When Persia was expanding toward Lydia, an oracle said, "If you attack Persia, a great empire will be destroyed." But he took that the wrong way and attacked Persia, and his own empire was completely destroyed. He was also a very wealthy king, so when the Persians conquered him, they became very rich. Herodotus noted that his gifts were preserved at Delphi.

Polycrates

Polycrates was the leader of a big fortified island in Ionia. Unfortunately for him, he got crucified. This happened because when the Persians expanded west, they couldn't conquer his super-fortified island fortress, so they decided to trick him. The Persians invited him to peace talks, then captured him and crucified him.

Crucifixion is when your hands are nailed onto a giant cross and the idea is that you either bleed out or die of thirst. Usually, this process takes several days to kill you. It's rather painful.

The First Invasion of Greece

Darius, the Persian king, sent two messengers to ask the Athenians for earth and water (asking them to surrender). One was sent to Athens, and the other to Sparta. After a few days, one messenger finally reached Athens.

"Why are you here?" the Athenians asked the messenger.

"I am here to ask for earth and water," the messenger replied. The Athenians looked like they were going to explode with anger. They buried him alive and shouted, "There's your earth!"

The second messenger arrived at Sparta and asked for earth and water. The soldiers threw him down a well, screaming in rage, "There's your water!"

Darius ordered one of his generals to gather an army of soldiers to defeat the Athenians, and the general said it would be easy to defeat them with the 200,000 men they gathered.

The army boarded the ships. Some of the ships carried cavalry, some archers, and others carried infantry. The general then yelled, "Set sail for Greece!"

Persian Soldier

Persian soldiers didn't have heavy armor. They had a wooden shield and a six foot long spear. It had a bronze spike at the back. The tip of the spear was made of iron, and they had small swords tucked in to a belt. They wore no helmets and had many more soldiers than the Athenians.

They finally saw Marathon and the general thought it would be the perfect place for the army to land.

The Athenian army, which was 20,000 soldiers, started to march to Marathon. They were led by the general Miltiades.

They finally arrived at Marathon, and they knew that the Persians wanted to fight them in the big open space below, but they wanted to fight the Persian army in a small and narrow space so that they would have a better chance of winning. The Athenian soldiers marched up a mountain, and found a place to set up camp. When they finished, they looked over the Persian camp, and their camp looked like a mouse compared to the Persians.

Greek Soldier

Greek soldiers had wooden shields, and large spears. The spear was made out of wood but the top was bronze and at the bottom there was a small bronze ball.

Persian Armor

The Persians, unlike the Greeks, had archers and they could fire from a long distance. They had light chain armor, and the high end elite-troops had bronze armor. Their shields were four feet in length and were made of wicker. The Immortals came after all the regular soldiers died or if the Persians were losing a battle. The archers' bows and arrows were based on the Scythian model.

Greek Armor

The Greeks had really heavy battle armor because they mostly fought hand to hand combat. The chestplates weighed forty pounds. Weapons like spears and swords couldn't easily penetrate the heavy armor the Greeks wore. The spears they used were called *Doru*. The *Doru* was about 7-8 feet long! The helmets protected the head a lot because a sword to the face could cause a massive injury or, even worse, death. The Spartans thought that countries who used archery or anything instead of sword fighting in battles were cowardly.

Sparta and Athens

Sparta and Athens were two cities in what we now call Greece. They were different in many ways. Sparta was located in the Peloponnesus, while Athens was part of the mainland. Sparta had two kings, but Athens was a democracy. Because of this, Sparta was very war-oriented (a boy's training began at seven years old).

Here, we show how Sparta and Athens reacted to the arrival of the Ionian king Aristagoras asking for more soldiers.

The Battle of Marathon

The Athenians knew that they were terribly outnumbered, so they sent a runner named Phidippides to run to Sparta, which was about 150 miles away. Phidippides got there in only thirty-six hours! When he arrived, he asked the Spartans to send reinforcements, but they were in the middle of a Spartan festival. So they said they would come by the next full moon. Phidippides ran back to the Athenian camp. When Phidippides told Miltiades the news, he was furious.

Then a soldier ran up to Miltiades, and said, "Sir, I was watching the Persian army. Their cavalry is gone."

Miltiades thanked the soldier, and told him, "We are going to attack and switch our strategy. Instead of having all three parts of our army with the same number of troops, we will thin out the middle and make the wings thicker."

When the Persians saw the Athenians, they quickly set up their army. The Athenians started marching down the hill. Once they were in range of the archers, they ran towards the Persians, yelling as loud as they could, because the Greeks knew that the Persian archers could destroy them if they kept marching.

The Persians saw how the middle of the Phalanx was weaker, and attacked that spot. Little did the Persians know that they were all marching into a trap.

The two sides of the Athenian army closed around the Persians, like barn doors closing. Soon it became a killing zone. The tide was starting to turn and they left a little hole for the Persians to run out. All of the Persians ran for the ships. The Athenians chased them, and burned as many ships as they could, but didn't get to all of them. The Persians set sail for Athens.

Phidippides ran back to Athens to give them the great news. When he got there he shouted, "We are victorious!" Then he dropped dead from exhaustion.

The Athenian soldiers marched back to Athens and they got there just in time to face the Persian ships. When the Persians got there and saw the Athenian army lined up along the tops of the cliffs, they knew they would lose, so they sailed back to Persia.

The Hoplite

Hoplites were Greek foot soldiers. They had one-meter diameter shields and 8 ft. long spears. They also had short swords for after their spears broke or got lost. The hoplite's armor consisted of a simple chest plate, greaves, and a helmet. The shields had one strap for their arms to go through and one for them to hold. Most of the Greeks had terrifying monster designs on their shields so it would scare their enemies, but the Spartans thought they were beyond that and just put Lambda on theirs.

Persian Ship

Persian ships had large sails, and in the back of the boat was a large purple Persian flag. There were small seats under the deck where the soldiers sat. The deck above had small railings about knee high. They floor was made of polished wood.

Hoplite Word Study

Hopl + ite → Hoplite

Definition: "Heavily armed ancient Greek foot soldier"

Part of speech: Noun

Root: Greek: *Hopla*

Denotation: "Arms and armor, gear for war."

Related word: Panoply

Miltiades

Miltiades was a Greek general who commanded the Greek army at the Battle of Marathon. He was the son of Cimon Coalemos I (an Olympic chariot-racer) and the father of Cimon II (an Athenian politician). His father was a wealthy man because of the Olympic chariot-racing. Miltiades, Cimon I, and Cimon II were part of the Philaid clan, who were rivals of the powerful Alcmaeonidae, but what Miltiades was most famous for was his ingenious strategy at the Battle of Marathon. He was elected to serve as one of the ten generals for 490 BCE., but the other generals knew that Miltiades was a brilliant commander and agreed to let him lead during the battle.

The Persian Interlude

Darius, the Persian king, was furious because he lost the Battle of Marathon, which was the first battle between Greece and Persia. Even though the Persian Empire had ten times as many soldiers as the Greeks, the Persians were defeated. Darius wanted to get back at Greece for defeating him.

Darius started to collect the biggest army in the whole world, just to defeat little Greece. The army was 2.5 million men, according to Herodotus.

The women worked to collect food for the army. Persians mostly ate meat and bread. The bread was made from wheat or barley. They also grew herbs and spices. They made stews for the army made from meat and fruit with herbs. Apricots, lemons, pistachios, and other food came to Europe through Persia. Other condiments and spices were used in Persian food.

War Elephant
The elephants were hired along with their riders as mercenary troops. They came from Indian lands under Persian rule.

They had to have enough cavalry and armor for everyone in the army. Everyone started to make swords, daggers, and bows and arrows for all to have weapons.

Two spies were sent from Greece to Persia to see what they was doing. The spies were caught and, instead of being killed, they were shown everything and then sent back. Darius did this so they would get intimidated when they saw his army.

In 486 BCE, Darius died, and his son, Xerxes, took over the empire. Egypt decided that maybe this new Persian king was not a good fighter, so they should just revolt against them. However Persia conquered them again, and Xerxes continued his father's plan for the invasion of Greece. Only this time, he would lead the army himself.

Persian Bow and Arrow
The Persian archers used them against the Greeks.

Xerxes

Xerxes was the king of Persia who ruled for twenty-one years, from 486 BC to 465 BC, when he was assassinated by one of his bodyguards. Xerxes wanted to take out Greece because before Xerxes was king, his dad (Darius I) was defeated by Greeks at the Battle of Marathon (even though his dad's army was ten times bigger).

Xerxes gathered a very big army to attack Greece, but there were downsides to having the biggest army ever created. For example, you need to have another army to carry food, messages, water, and animals. The army also had to sack every town they came to because they needed more food. The generals also couldn't communicate with the army very well while they were fighting. They couldn't exactly shout to the whole army because they would give their plan away, and it was so loud no one could hear them. The generals had to have messengers to communicate with the army.

When they set up camp, Xerxes had his own tent-palace that the Persians brought when they went to war, which was carried from camp to camp. The perimeter of the mini-palace was 700 meters. He was the king, so of course he had to have his family with him, as well as couches, beds, servants, slaves, and his own personal cattle.

Map of Persian Empire

Persian conquered almost everything around them. They kept expanding and expanding and conquering.

Interlude Word Study

Inter + lude → Interlude
Definition: Pause between two parts
Part of speech: Noun
Root: Latin: *ludus*
Denotation: "A play"
Related words: ludicrous, elude, collude, delude, collusion

Army Word Study

Arm + y → Army
Definition: "Military land force"
Part of speech: Noun
Root: Latin: *Arma*
Denotation: "Tools, weapons"
Related words: armadillo, armoire, armada

The Greek Interlude

The Interlude was a time when the Greeks and Persians were at a standstill in the Greco-Persian wars. The pause was caused by the Persians gathering the largest army the world had ever seen. On the Greek side of the Interlude, Themistocles became the archon of Athens, which was like president. Later the Greeks found a silver mine at Laurion. Themistocles convinced the Athenians to build 200 triremes with their money.

Triremes were warships with bronze rams at the front and a big curve at the back. To use the ram, they would have to have extremely good maneuvering skills to hit the side of the enemy ship. It had a crew of 200 men, and 170 of them were rowers. The commanders were called trierarchs.

The bow and the outriggers were reinforced for ramming. The triremes went 9 kilometers per hour over long distances, and over short distances, they went 12-15 KPH. On the lowest level of the ship, there were twenty-seven rowers on each side. The middle level of rowers also had twenty-seven rowers on each side. There were thirty-one rowers on each side on the top.

There was also one person at the stern of the ship using two broad oars to steer the ship. The trireme evolved from the bireme, which was basically just a trireme with two decks instead of three. The oars were between 4 and 4.5 meters long. At the outrigger level, the ship was six meters wide; at the bottom, it was three, and it was thirty-seven meters long.

Spartan Warriors

The Spartans were the greatest warriors the world had ever seen. The Spartan women said, "Come back with your shield or on it!" meaning win or die.

The Greco-Persian Wars were the start of the Hellenic League, which was an alliance between around thirty of the southern city-states against Persia, created about 485 BCE. During the Interlude, the Greeks were squabbling over who would be the leader of the army that they were creating to stop Persia.

They were also fighting over where and when they would meet the Persians. The Greeks called a big meeting to get to know other city-states and end any feuds, with their common interest at the heart of the decision. Calling themselves

Armor

Greek body armor, leg armor, and helmet.

the League of the Greeks or the Hellenic League, they made Sparta the leader of all their collective forces.

At first, they considered collecting their troops at the Isthmus of Corinth, a narrow piece of land connecting the Peloponnese to the rest of Greece, but this plan was rejected by the Athenians because it would have abandoned Central Greece to the enemy. They finally decided upon the narrow valley of Thermopylae (read about the battle of Thermopylae on page 16).

Greek Weapons

Sword: A straight blade quite similar to the Japanese short sword, The sword was a secondary weapon made for use in case the spear was lost or broken. The sword was used by the Greeks for close range fighting. It was called a *Xiphos*.

Spear: The spear was eight feet long and one and a half inches in diameter. The main blade was leaf-shaped. It had a point on the bottom used for sticking into the ground to stab opponents. The point was smaller from the main top one. The Greeks mainly threw it, so it was generally a one-use weapon, but they also used it for stabbing.

Shield: The shield was thirty pounds, three feet in diameter, and it usually had a face on the front to scare the enemy away. The Spartans were so powerful that they put a single Lambda(Λ), which was a Greek letter, on their shield and scared their enemies because the enemies knew that they were battling the Spartans and they were the best.

Bireme

A bireme was a Greek ship with two levels of oars. It was the predecessor of the trireme.

Greek Pickaxe

This is a pickaxe that could have been used by the silver miners at Laurion.

The Battle of Thermopylae Background

It was 480 BCE. The Greeks had won the last battle, and it was time for a second. It was called the Battle of Thermopylae because the pass they battled in was called Thermopylae, famous for its hot springs. The Greek army picked this spot because it was a narrow valley. They preferred to have their battles in narrow places because the Persians had a very large army, which made it hard for the Persians to fit all of their army in a narrow valley at one time, so they could not have strength in numbers.

The Greeks sent an army of about 7,000 people. The Persians were about a hundred times bigger. So, obviously, the Greeks were the underdog. The Greek force included 300 Spartan soldiers. The Greeks had great skill in moving together as a unit. The Persians were armed with lots of men with bows. The Spartans held one value above all other, and that was warfare. At birth, if there was a Spartan baby that was weak, it was abandoned and left to die. At the age of seven, the Spartan boys would go to military school to prepare for when they would go to war when they were older. They joined the army full-time at twenty.

Barbarians!

The Greeks and Persians thought each other to be barbaric, and were constantly blaming each other for something. They also thought that the other side was always wrong. One way they thought each other to be barbaric was that Greeks thought that it was barbaric to encase limbs inside clothing, while Persians thought it was barbaric to not have clothes on. Greeks also thought that everyone who wasn't Greek was barbaric.

Underdog Word Study

Under + dog → Underdog

Definition: A person or an animal that is predicted to lose.

Under root: under

Dog root: docga

Under language of origin: Old English

Dog language of origin: Old English

Denotation: "the beaten dog in a fight"

Under part of speech: preposition

Dog part of speech: noun

Greek tent

Greek Helmet

It had feathers that were shooting up on the back of the helmet.

Map of Greece

Thermopylae is right in the middle.

The Battle of Thermopylae

When the Persians and the Greeks met at Thermopylae, it took *four whole days* for the Persians to arrive, because they had such a big army. Leonidas went with the Greek army. He was one of the two kings of Sparta. Before the battle, the Persians called out, "Surrender your weapons!" and the Greeks yelled back, "Come and get them!"

The first day, the Persians sent some people to go check on the Spartans. They came back to Xerxes and said, "All they're doing is combing their hair?" The whole Persian army was laughing, except for one general. He turned pale and said, "They're trying to look their best for the Underworld. They're getting ready to fight to the death."

Now you should know who the underdog was. If you don't know, here's a hint: The Greeks had a few thousand soldiers. The Persians had around a hundred times that or more. Helpful? The Spartans and the Persians had both been waiting for each other to attack. Then the Persians started advancing towards the Greeks. The Spartans were destroying the Persians like a lawn mower, cutting the Persians in half.

On the Greek side, there was a shepherd who knew about a secret path through the mountains that led to the back end of the Greek army. His name was Ephialtes. He was probably thinking, *Hmm, the Persians are this huge empire, and we're just an ant compared to them. Maybe I should switch to their side.* That's exactly what he did! He betrayed the Greek army and told the Persians about the path.

"Go home," Leonidas told the Athenians and the other city-states when he found out. At this point, the Greeks knew they could never win. So all the other city-states went home, leaving three hundred Spartans. The Persians marched up the path, single file, and surrounded the Spartan army.

During the last day of the battle, Leonidas was killed, and his men were fighting over the body. The Spartans were finally defeated by the Persians raining down arrows and spears on them. Even though the Persians won, they had lost so many men it seemed as if they were defeated.

> **Reinforcements Word Study**
> Re + in + force + ment + s → Reinforcements
> Definition: "Extra supporting soldiers"
> Part of speech: Noun
> Root: Latin: *fortis*
> Denotation: "Strong, mighty"
> Related words: force, fortitude, fortress

The Secret Path

This is a view of the secret path Ephialtes told the Persians about. It was a path the Persians didn't know about and that path would lead them behind the Greeks. If the Persians went up the path, the Greeks would be surrounded and destroyed..

Leonidas

Leonidas was one of the two Spartan kings. The two kings were responsible for two different aspects of Sparta. Leonidas led the Spartan army to war, and the other king stayed in Sparta and ran the city-state.

During the Greco-Persian Wars Leonidas played a big part because the Spartans were some of the Greeks' best warriors. Leonidas was a fearless leader, until he was killed by the Persians at the Battle of Thermopylae. He died after the rest of the Greek army left, and the Spartans were the only soldiers left at the battleground. He was so important to the Spartans that they fought over his dead body with the Persians.

His last stand with the other Spartans made a big impact on the Greco-Persian Wars because it slowed down the Persian assault on Greece and bought the Greeks some time to prepare for the oncoming attack.

Persian Archer

The Persians were furious that the Spartans weren't destroyed yet. So they stepped back and let the archers shower the remaining Spartans with arrows. Two hundred and ninety-nine Spartans were killed from this. The sole survivor, unconscious, woke up, realized he was the only survivor, then committed suicide. Three hundred Spartans were lost. 20,000 Persians were killed The Spartans had no archers because they thought it was a weapon for the cowardly.

The Persians Head Towards Athens

After the Battle of Thermopylae (see page 16), the Persians marched south and decided to invade Athens with their whole army. The Athenians couldn't do anything because their army was so small and no other Greek cities wanted to help. Athens was probably the most beautiful city state in Greece. It had beautiful temples and houses, so when Athens was destroyed and burned down all the Athenians were very sad because that was their home and they grew up in it.

The Athenians went to the Oracle of Delphi for advice because they knew the Persians were coming (the Oracle of Delphi was a place where a priestess gave prophecies, mainly from Apollo), and the Oracle said that the Persians would sack Athens and the Athenians should flee. The Athenians were going to abandon Athens, but they went back to the Oracle to maybe get a different prophecy. But it still said to get out of Athens. Fortunately it also said that Athena begged Zeus to help the Athenians (this is only one translation of the prophecy, there are many): "Pallas Athena is not able to move Olympian Zeus with entreaty and counsel of wisdom. Far-seeing Zeus, however, bequeaths a wall of wood to the Triton-born goddess, alone impregnable, which will save you and your children. Remain not waiting for the horsemen and foot soldiers coming in hosts from Asia, but turn your back and withdraw. Verily, a day will arrive when you can meet them. Divine Salamis, you will cause the death of women's sons, whether Demeter is scattered or gathered in."

The Greeks did what they always did: they argued, because they didn't know what the prophecy meant. Some thought it meant that they had to stay and put up hedges. They thought that would protect Athens but they were wrong and they were killed when the Persians arrived. One Greek family said, "Maybe we should surrender because they have a bigger army than us." For that, they were stoned to death (which means people threw rocks at them until they died).

Totalitarianism Word Study

Total + i + tare + ian + ism → Totalitarianism

Definition: "A system of government that is only run by one ruler."

Part of speech: Noun
Root: Latin: *Totus*
Denotation: "All at once, whole, entire"
Related Words: total, subtotal, totality

Map of Greece

Labels on map: Pass of Thermopylae, Delphi, Salamis, Athens, Sparta, Aegean Sea

Key
=Neutrals
=pass of Thermopylae
=Athens and allies
=Sparta and allies

Themistocles

Themistocles was the one of the Archons of Athens during the Greco-Persian Wars. An Archon was one of the nine chief magistrates of Athens. During the war he fought at the Battle of Marathon. He was the one who persuaded the Athenians to use the silver that they found to pay to build 200 triremes. At the Battle of Salamis he was essentially in control of the Greek navy.

He ordered Athens to be rebuilt to be a bigger, better city after the Sack of Athens but Sparta got upset. After the war he was exiled to Argos. He fled Greece and went to Asia Minor. He became governor of Magnesia and lived the rest of his life there.

Map of Greece - Key
Green= Neutrals
Blue= Pass of Thermopylae
Orange= Athens and Allies
Yellow= Sparta and Allies

Oracle Word Study
Ora + cle → Oracle
Definition: "Place or person that gives messages and prophecies from the god Apollo."
Part of speech: Noun
Root: Latin: *Orare*
Denotation: "Pray, plead."
Related words: oratory, adore, inexorable

The Sack of Athens

The sack of Athens happened in 480 BCE. Most of the Athenians fled Athens as the Persians approached, and spread out across Greece (mostly in the Peloponnese because the Persians controlled most of the mainland). Many of the Athenians went to the island of Salamis, which was across the Straits of Salamis from Athens, and waited for the Persians. After some of the Athenians reached Salamis they could see the huge Persian army coming and watched as the Persians burned their city and their homes to the ground. We now use the term "sacked" in football when the quarterback gets sacked by a defensive lineman and it almost means the same thing but instead a city gets sacked, which means that it is destroyed and burned to the ground.

Themistocles went to Sparta to talk about what they should do now that Athens was

The Dog Story
When Themistocles's dad and family were evacuating to Salamis, the boat was filled up completely so they could not take their dog, but the dog swam next to them all the way to Salamis, but when they arrived the dog was so exhausted that (like Phidippides the runner) he died.

sacked. Before Athens was sacked the Athenians had discovered silver deposits. Themistocles had the idea to invest they money from the silver mines in 200 triremes for the Athenian navy (see page 14). Now, Themistocles used those ships to threaten the Spartans, because the Spartans wanted to defend at Isthmia (which was right above Corinth on the isthmus that connects mainland Greece with the Peloponnese). But Themistocles wanted to defend at Salamis, because of the prophecy about the wooden walls (see page 20). Themistocles thought that the "wooden walls" prophecy meant a wall of ships, and that they should make their stand at an island called Salamis which was near Athens, so he threatened to leave with the Athenian navy if they didn't. That led to the Battle of Salamis.

The Sack of Athens

When Athens was burned down, it was a horrifying sight. The Athenians were devastated, but it meant that they would eventually rebuild Athens to look even more beautiful and build more temples for the gods when the wars were over.

Herodotus

Herodotus was a Greek historian who lived during the 5th century BCE. He was born in 485 BCE. As a child, he lived in Halicarnassus, which is a Greek city state in southwest Asia.

His Mother was Dryo and his Father was Lyxes. His brothers were Theodorus and Democritus.

He was known as "The Father of History" because he did a lot of documenting and writing about the Greco-Persian Wars. He was famous for that because he did it very systematically.

We believe that Herodotus passed away in 425 BCE at age 60. He died in Thurii, in Italy.

Beautiful Attica

Attica was one of the biggest city-states in Greece, and also the most democratic. Athens was always the bravest (not counting Sparta) and the first to protect Greece. Athens also built amazing temples, such as the Parthenon and the whole Acropolis, which you can visit today. Right now Athens is the capital of Greece.

The Battle of Salamis

As the hot sun shone upon the infuriated Greeks' backs, they were as mad as an exploding volcano. Athens, one of their city-states, had been sacked.

In August, 480 BCE, some of the Athenians had fled to an island called Salamis, right before Athens was burned. It was destroyed because the Greeks lost the Battle of Thermopylae. If they had won, the huge army of Persian men wouldn't have been able to burn down Athens.

The Persian navy was waiting outside the straits between Athens, Salamis, and the Mediterranean Sea. The Greek navy was waiting in a small bay on the island of Salamis. They waited for eleven days because the space the Greeks had was an advantage to the Greek navy and because the space the Persians had was an advantage to the Persian navy.

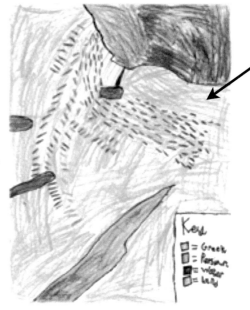

One of the Greeks' best generals, Themistocles, ordered a servant to go to Xerxes and tell him a lie: "I come from Themistocles, and he is secretly on your side. I want to say that the Greeks are going up north towards Eleusina and I think you should follow them." Xerxes fell for the trick. He told his navy to chase them, and they did. The Persian ships in the narrow channel had difficulty in turning to meet the Greeks and the right side picked up speed and went faster than the left side, which left their sides exposed.

Themistocles knew that there were swells, times when a wave comes through the strait, so he told his navy to get aligned with the wind, and the wind changed right behind the Greeks, so they had rowers, swells, and wind as they rammed the Persian ships. The Persians who didn't get rammed tried to run away, but the Greeks ships from the island of Aegina blocked their way, so the Persians were all boxed in. The Persians had to fight their way back out, and they did. They got out, and retreated to Lamia. The Greeks won the Battle of Salamis.

Triremes

The Greeks had about 300 before the Battle of Salamis. A trireme was a type of ancient warship that had three rows of rowers on the bottom, and a platform above for the soldiers to run onto the enemy ships.

How Persians were Exposed

This is how the Persians were exposed. It shows how the right side went faster than the left. The purple was the Persians, and the green was the Greeks.

Artemisia

Who was Artemisia? She was the only woman who fought in the Greco-Persian Wars. She was a Persian commander and a captain in the battle of Salamis. When Xerxes saw his marines being smashed by the Greeks, he noticed that only a few of Artemisia's ships crashed, and that she was doing a better job of commanding than the men. He said, "My men have become women and my women have become men."

There is not a lot known about Artemisia, but we know her name is Greek. In Greek her name means Gift from Artemis.

She was born in Halicarnassus, Turkey, and died in Lefkada, Greece. Her child was Pisindelis, her father was Lygdamis, and her mother was Prudentia.

Trireme Word Study

Tri + reme → Trireme
Definition: A Greek warship with three rows of oars.
Part of speech: Noun
Roots: Tri and Remus
Language of origin: Latin: "Three" and "Oar"
Related words: trifocal, trilateral, tricycle, triangle

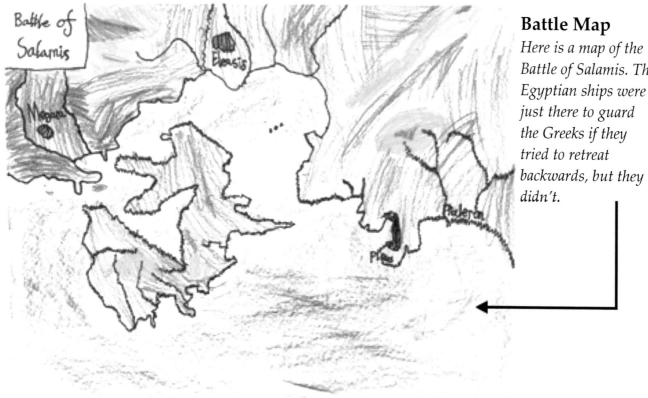

Battle of Salamis

Battle Map

Here is a map of the Battle of Salamis. The Egyptian ships were just there to guard the Greeks if they tried to retreat backwards, but they didn't.

The Battle of Plataea

Xerxes and most of the Persian army went away, leaving the best troops behind, and he left the Persian general, Mardonius, in charge. Mardonius and army retreated to northern Thebes for the winter. When spring came, they moved south to Plataea, because that was one of the places that was big enough for the massive Persian army.

The Greeks made the biggest army they had ever made so far. It contained about 38,000 hoplites, with 70,000 support troops. The Persian army had at least three times as many soldiers as the Greeks.

Finally the Greeks decided to attack. They ran in their phalanx formation towards the Persian Camp. Mardonius

Persian Archers

ordered the Persian archers to fire a volley of arrows at the Greeks. The Greeks ran back and dodged the arrows. Since the Greeks were moving back, Mardonius thought the Greeks were fully retreating. Now the real battle began.

The Persian army marched forward but they didn't know that there were depressions scattered around the battlefield. Unluckily enough, they ran into a depression. While the front started climbing out of the depression, the Persians in the back were running as fast as they could and the soldiers bunched up.

The Spartans closed in on all sides of the depression and attacked with no mercy, killing a ton of Persians. The Greeks were mad. "Revenge for Athens, we take no prisoners!" was what they said. See page 22 for more on the Sack of Athens.

The Spartans were incredibly good at fighting hand to hand because Spartan kids at the age of seven were taken away from their homes to train for battle. The Spartans usually fought like it was easy. During the battle, a Spartan lost all his weapons and threw a rock, hoping to hit a soldier. He was quite lucky and hit Mardonius, the Persian commander, on the forehead, killing him. With no leader, the Persians went crazy, and fled from the Greeks, but the Greeks followed them. Some lucky Persians escaped, and barely survived.

Weapons and Armor

Monuments

The Greeks created monuments to commemorate their dead soldiers. They named most of the monuments after their battles. "Tell the Spartans, you who pass us by, that here in obedience to their laws we lie," was a poem written by Simonides of Ceos, and was carved into a monument that was built right after the Battle of Thermopylae, in memory of Leonidas and the 300 Spartans who died during the battle. They also made a monument out of the melted weapons of the Persian soldiers who were defeated. It was called the Serpent Column, Serpentine Column, Plataean Tripod, or Delphi Tripod. It's still called that today. It was to commemorate the Greeks who fought and were killed, yet defeated the Persian Empire at the Battle of Plataea.

Revenge Word Study

Re + venge → Revenge

Definition: "Inflicting harm as payback for a wrong suffered"

Part of speech: Noun

Root: Latin: *Vindicare*

Denotation: "To lay claim to"

Related Words: avenge, vengeance, vindication, avenger, vengeful

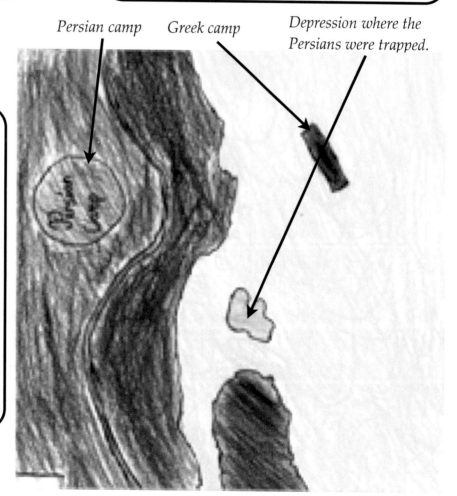

Persian camp   *Greek camp*   *Depression where the Persians were trapped.*

Living in the Golden Age

The Golden Age, also known as the Age of Pericles, was in Athens, Greece. Athens was the main city in Greece. The city was named after Athena, their patron goddess. Athena was the goddess of wisdom and military victory. Athens was the largest and most powerful city state. The name Athens came about because there was a contest between Athena and Poseidon (god of the sea), and Poseidon promised the riches of the sea while Athena gave them the gift of the olive tree. The Athenians decided the olive tree was better, so Athena became the patron of Athens and Athens was named after her.

The Golden Age was the renewing of Athens after it had been sacked by the Persians. It was the time when much of our present day culture was invented or developed further, such as music, math and algebra, government, philosophy, art, literature, architecture, sculpture, and, of course, the Acropolis, standing forty feet tall. It was the beginning of Western civilization. It had come out of their dark ages, which is why it is called The Golden Age.

Athena

This was what Goddess of Wisdom, Athena, looked like. She is carrying her shield.

They had a lot of brilliant people living at the same time in the Golden Age including Socrates, Plato, Aristotle, Herodotus, Themistocles, Aristophanes, Xenophon, Pericles, Aeschylus, Sophocles, and Euripides. Aeschylus, Sophocles, and Euripides were three of the main people who invented drama. People think their plays were even as good as Shakespeare! Socrates, Plato, and Aristotle worked on math and philosophy.

Archimedes, who lived after the Golden Age was a mathematician. He believed in the monad power (the power that the numeral one can do everything) though it happened that he was incorrect and the numeral one could not do everything. Archimedes was devastated but he did not give up. He also was the most-famous mathematician and inventor in ancient Greece. Though sadly one day he was so focused on his math work he did not notice when a soldier came in to murder him in c. 212 BC, during the Second Punic War, when Roman forces under General Marcus Claudius Marcellus captured the city of Syracuse. Though overall Archimedes was a great guy, he thought women were only for doing laundry, making food, and staying at home.

The Golden Age was a time for economic growth and cultural celebrations. It was a time of smart people in all subjects and was the starting time of many things in the world today, even though the Golden Age only lasted for fifty years.

Golden Age Greece

This is where the Golden Age, also known as The Age of Pericles, was centered, in the city of Athens.

Archimedes

This was Archimedes! He was a very famous mathematician, and he was super smart. He was very involved with the number "one."

Persian Empire (Now Turkey)

Athens

Sparta

Mediterranean Sea

Crete

Philosophy Word Study

Phile + o + soph + y → Philosophy

Definition: The study of the world, reality, and existence.

Part of Speech: Noun

Roots: Greek: *Philos* and *Sophia*

Denotation: "Friend, lover" and "Knowledge, wisdom"

Related words: bibliophile, sophomore, sophisticated

Inventions in the Golden Age

One of the greatest things the Athenians invented in the Golden Age was drama. Drama is a big part of our modern day civilization. One of the biggest and most famous theaters the Athenians made was the theatre of Dionysus Eleuthereus. Sitting on the south slope of the Acropolis, the theatre of Dionysus Eleuthereus was one of the main theaters of the Golden Age.

The Athenians also made big things, including the Acropolis and the whole renewing of Athens. It must have taken a lot of hard work to make Athens all over again.

Then the Athenians began minting their own money and using coins. Most coins had an owl, the sacred bird of Athena, who was the patron of Athens. They had Dekadrachm, which were worth ten drachma and weighed forty-three grams, Tetradrachm, which were worth four Drachma and weighed 17.5 grams, Didrachm, which were worth two Drachma, Drachma, Tetrobol, Triobol, Diobol, Obol, Tritartemorion, and on and on and on. The Dekadrachm and the Tetradrachm were the most commonly used coins in ancient Greece.

Coins

These were some of the ancient coins, the owl was the sacred bird of Athena, Goddess of Wisdom who was the patron of Athens.

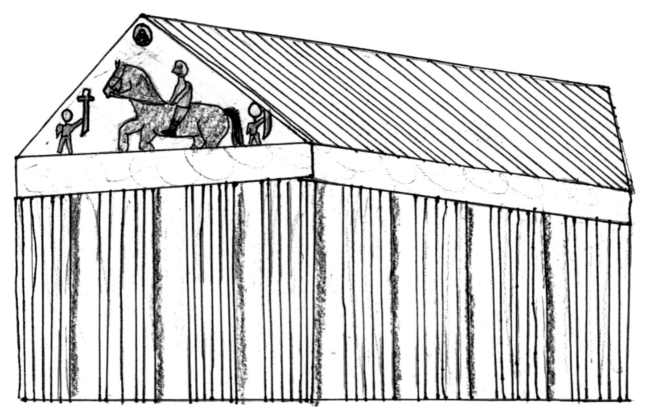

The Parthenon

This is the Parthenon that stood proudly on the Acropolis. It was one of the many buildings they built on the Acropolis. It was mostly made out of limestone, and the interior had a golden statue of Athena and her minor goddess, Nike. The Parthenon still stands on the Acropolis in Athens today!

A Vase

This vase is one of the artifacts they made back in The Golden Age. It is a red-figure vase, meaning only the black was painted and the figures in red were the natural color of the clay.

Invention Word Study

In + vent + ion → Invention

Definition: Something new someone has made

Part of Speech: Noun

Roots: Latin: *Venire*

Denotation: "To come"

Related words: inventor, adventure, convenient

Conclusion

After the Greco-Persian Wars and the Golden Age of Greece there were many new inventions that changed the course of history. Without the Greco-Persian Wars, life would be substantially different from what it is now.

If the Persians had won, the ways that we live today would be different — not better or worse, just different. If they had conquered Greece, the Persian way of life would have spread to Europe. If the Persians had won, then this book probably wouldn't be here. And then again, if the Persians had won, we would be glad those stupid Greeks hadn't won.

Sadly, about fifty years after the Greco-Persian Wars, another war started, called the Peloponnesian War. It was a war between Sparta and Athens. The Peloponnesian War was a Pyrrhic victory for Sparta. A Pyrrhic victory is when you win but you lose so many people it's hardly worth it. The Peloponnesian War is also known as the Suicide of Greece, and it was the end of the Golden Age of Greece.

A big thanks to the readers who have bought this book, and a message to any kid who might be reading: If you have an idea for a project like this, tell your teacher and show them this book. Never let your dreams stay dreams. You can make a change.

All profits from this book go to treatment systems to provide clean water to a school or orphanage that doesn't have it. 780 million people don't have clean water -- that's about 10.5 percent of the world! We really appreciate you buying this book. See what difference kids can make?

Thanks,
The Nueva 4th Graders of 2017-2018

Resources

We couldn't find any books for kids about the Greco-Persian Wars, which is why we wrote this book. In order to get this information, we had to use all of these books and websites.

Books

Anonymous. *The Rise and Fall of the Persian Empire*. Newark: Speedy Publishing. 2017.

Bowra, C. M.. *Classical* Greece. New York: Time, Inc., 1965.

Burell, Roy. *The Greeks*. New York: Oxford University Press, 1989.

Connolly, Peter. *The Greek Armies*. Macdonald Educational, 1977.

Durant, Will. *The Life of Greece*. New York: Simon & Schuster, 1939.

Fields, Nic. *Thermopylae 480 BC*. New York: Osprey Publishing, 2007.

Herodotus. *The Histories*. Translated by A.D. Godley. New York: G.P. Putnam's Sons, 1930.

Markham, Lois. *Ancient Persia*. New York: Kids Discover, 2006.

Peach, Susan and Anne Mallard. *The Greeks*. London: Usborne Publishing, 1990.

Schlesinger, Arthur. *Xerxes*. Chicago: Chelsea House, 1987.

Middleton, Haydn. *Ancient Greece: War and Weapons*. Chicago: Reed Educational, 2003.

Pearson, Anne. *Ancient Greece*. New York: DK Publishing, 2007.

Scarborough, John. *Facets of Hellenic Life*. Boston: Houghton Mifflin, 1976.

Shepherd, William. *Plataea 479 BC*. Long Island City: Osprey Publishing, 2012.

Shepherd, William. *Salamis 480 BC*. Long Island City: Osprey Publishing, 2010.

Websites

ahistoryofgreece.com/goldenage.htm

ancient.eu

ancientathens.org/wars/trireme-ships-fleet-athens

ancientgreekarmor.weebly.com/shin-guards.html

ancientgreekbattles.net

ancientresource.com

britannica.com

classroom.synonym.com/ancient-greek-armor-weapons-during-battle-thermopylae-12579.html

commons.wikimedia.org

deadliestblogpage.files.wordpress.com

ducksters.com/history/ancient_greek_famous_people.php

ehistory.osu.edu/articles/ionian-revolt

en.wikibooks.org/wiki/Wikijunior:Ancient_Civilizations/Persians

en.wikipedia.org

etymonline.com

greekboston.com/wp-content/uploads/2016/07/Acroplis-Athens

hiistorysodope.blogspot.com/2007/12/golden-age-of-acient-greece-what-did.html

historymuseum.ca/cmc/exhibitions/civil/greece/gr1050e.shtml

historynet.com/the-end-of-athens.htm

hubpages.com/education/Ancient-Greece-The-Mycenaeans

i.pinimg.com/originals/

image.slidesharecdn.com/ancientgreece-141028192441-conversion-gate02/95/ancient-greece-world-history

img00.deviantart.net

indiansteelhandicrafts.com/product/ancient-greek-antique-armor/

kidsdiscover.com/wp-content/uploads/2014/03/Greek_Trireme.png

livius.org

militaryfactory.com/ancient-warfare/spartan-hoplite.asp

molossia.org/milacademy/Salamis.html

nationsonline.org

ontheworldmap.com/greece/islands/samos/samos-tourist-map.jpg

pbs.org/empires/thegreeks/background/

perseus.tufts.edu/Herakles/athena.html

primaryhomeworkhelp.co.uk/greece/athens.htm

quora.com/What-did-ancient-Greek-soldiers-wear-during-combat

realmofhistory.com/2016/01/19/10-things-you-may-not-have-known-about-the-greek-hoplites/

reddit.com/r/AskHistorians/comments/5cqh74/what_actually_happens_when_a_city_is_sacked/

runnersworld.com/motivation/the-real-pheidippides-story

spartacus.wikia.com/wiki/Hoplon

study.com/academy/lesson/battle-of-marathon-summary-facts-map.html

surveyworldhistory.com

thefamouspeople.com/greek-leaders.php

thefinertimes.com/Ancient-Wars/battle-of-Salamis.html

thegoldenageofathens.weebly.com

theidlewoman.files.wordpress.com

thoughtco.com/persian-wars-battle-of-Salamis

tripadvisor.com/LocationPhotoDirectLink-g644219-d10639852-i267463376-Pythagoras_Statue-Pythagorion_Samos_Northeast_Aegean_Islands.html

unc.edu/courses

web.wpi.edu/academics

webmd.com/asthma/guide/hypoxia-hypoxemia

Authors

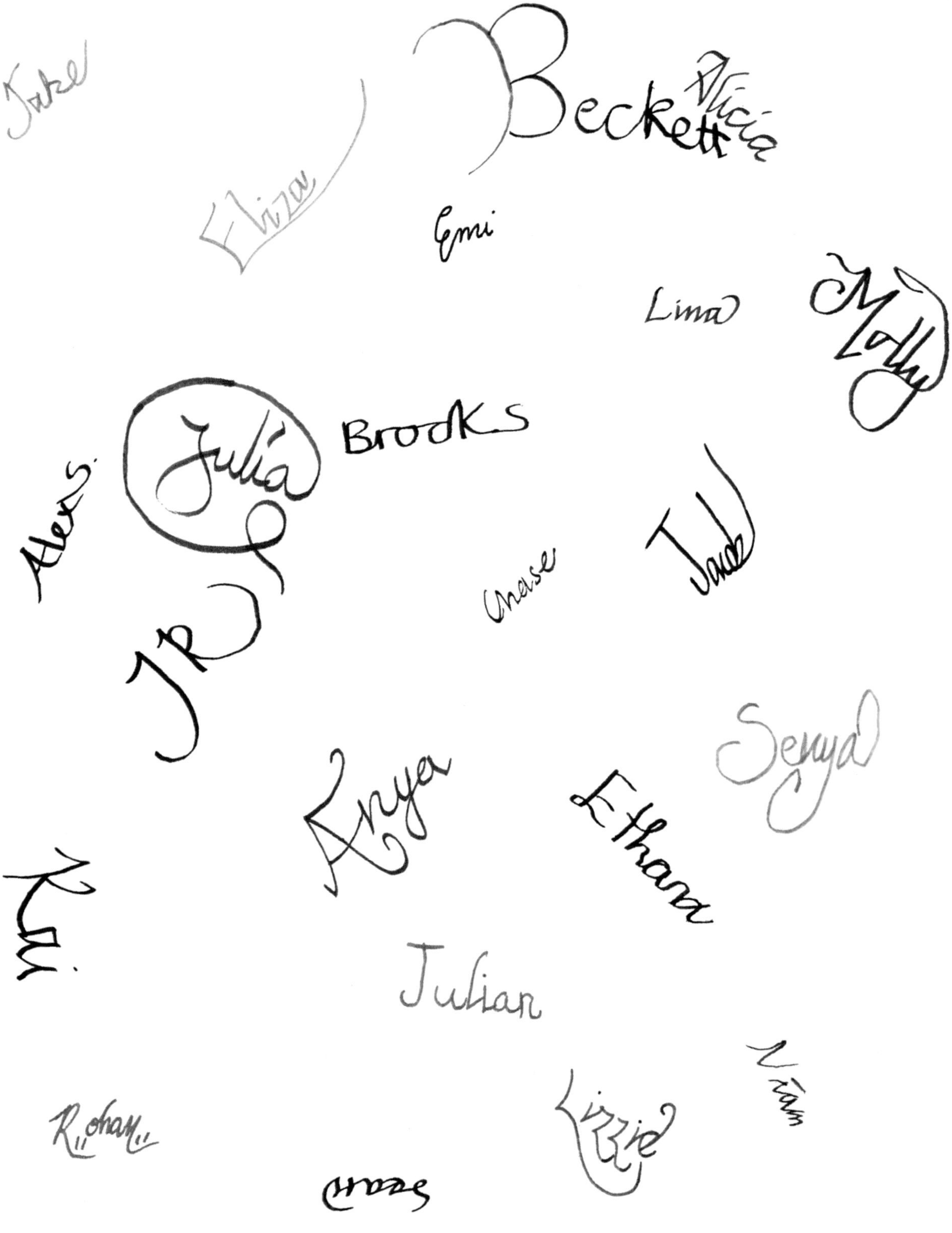

Jake

Eliza

Beckett

Alicia

Emi

Lima

Molly

Alexs.

Julia

Brooks

JR

Chase

Jack

Senyd

Anya

Ethan

Kai

Julian

Liam

Roham

Lizzie

Sean

Authors

Anna

Paige

Anton

Charlotte

Audra

Anne

Mylie

Ryan

Jack

Ava

Aryan

Nate

Katja

RJ

Alex

Eolin

Ellie

Rudy

David

Caleb

Laïga

Madison

36

26142535R00024

Made in the USA
San Bernardino, CA
15 February 2019